Dynamics of Identity
in the World of the
Early Christians

Dynamics of Identity in the World of the Early Christians

Associations, Judeans, and Cultural Minorities

Philip A. Harland

t&t clark

NEW YORK • LONDON

2009

The Continuum International Publishing Group Inc
80 Maiden Lane, New York, NY 10038

The Continuum International Publishing Group Ltd
The Tower Building, 11 York Road, London SE1 7NX

www.continuumbooks.com

Library of Congress Cataloging-in-Publication Data

A catalog record for this book is available from the Library of Congress.

Printed in the United States of America

ISBN-13: 9780567613288
ISBN-13: 9780567111463

For Cheryl, Nathaniel, and Justin

Contents

Illustrations ix

Preface xi

Map: Italy and the Eastern Roman Empire xiv

Introduction 1

Part 1: Judean and Christian Identities in the Context of Associations 23

1. Associations and Group Identity among Judeans and Christians 25

2. Local Cultural Life and Christian Identity: "Christ-Bearers"
   and "Fellow-Initiates" 47

Part 2: Familial Dimensions of Group Identity 61

3. "Brothers" in Associations and Congregations 63

4. "Mothers" and "Fathers" in Associations and Synagogues 82

Part 3: Identity and Acculturation among Judeans and Other Ethnic Associations 97

5. Other Diasporas: Immigrants, Ethnic Identities, and Acculturation 99

6. Interaction and Integration: Judean Families and Guilds at Hierapolis 123

Part 4: Group Interactions and Rivalries 143

7. Group Rivalries and Multiple Identities: Associations at Sardis and Smyrna 145

8. Perceptions of Cultural Minorities: Anti-Associations and their Banquets 161

Conclusion 182

Contents

Abbreviations   186

Bibliography
   1.   Epigraphic and Papyrological Collections   189
   2.   Other Primary and Secondary Sources   196

Indices
  Ancient Sources   220
  Inscriptions and Papyri   224
  Modern Authors   233
  Names, Places, and Subjects   237

Illustrations

1   Banqueting hall of the cowherds at Pergamon (second cent. CE)   30

2   Monument depicting three gods (Zeus, Artemis, and Apollo),
    an association, and entertainment, from Panormos near Kyzikos,
    now in British Museum (*GIBM* IV. 1007)   31

3   Monument set up by fishermen and fishmongers at Ephesos,
    now in the Selçuk Archaeological Museum (*IEph* 20; 50s CE)   34

4   Relief of Demeter from Kozçesme in northwestern Asia Minor,
    now in the Istanbul Archaeological Museum (fourth cent. BCE)   50

5   Statue of Dionysos, now in the Selçuk Archaeological Museum   51

6   Relief depicting a procession of a maenad and two satyrs,
    from Villa Quintilliana near Rome, now in the British Museum
    (ca. 100 CE)   53

7   Statue of Artemis of Ephesos, now in the Selçuk Archaeological Museum   55

8   Bronze statue of an athlete scraping oil from his body in connection
    with a competition, now in the Ephesos Museum, Vienna (Roman copy
    of a Greek original from ca. 320 BCE)   78

9   Bronze lamp depicting Herakles (often patron deity of athletes)
    fighting a centaur, now in the Ephesos Museum, Vienna (ca. 150–100 BCE)   79

10 Statue of Silenos caring for the baby Dionysos, now in the Louvre   93

11 Monument from Delos dedicated "to Apollo and the Italian gods"
    by the Italian Hermaists, Apolloniasts, and Poseidoniasts, now
    in the British Museum (*GIBM* IV 963 = *IDelosChoix* 157; 74 BCE)   105

12 Marble relief of Bendis, goddess of the Thracians, along with
    several athletic youths, now in the British Museum (ca. 400–375 BCE)   107

13 Grave "of the Judeans" from Hierapolis, with a menorah and lion
(*IHierapMir* 6 = *IJO* II 187)   125

14 Grave mentioning the "people of the Judeans" at Hierapolis
(*IHierapMir* 5 = *IJO* II 206)   126

15 Grave of P. Aelius Glykon and Aurelia Amia, involving guilds
of carpet-weavers and purple-dyers (*IHierapMir* 23 = *IJO* II 196)   129

16 Synagogue hall within the bath–gymnasium complex at Sardis   147

17 Statue head of Herodes Atticus, now in the British Museum   155

18 The meeting place of the builders' guild at Ostia   157

19 Architrave depicting a struggle between a Lapith and Centaur,
from the Parthenon at Athens, now in the British Museum
(fifth cent. BCE)   164

20 Sketch of the rules of the Bacchic association (Iobacchoi) at Athens,
from Harrison 1906, figure 25   173